Chicken ~~à~~

Tales of an Air Steward

Jim Barham

Published by Pomegranate Press,
Dolphin House, 51 St Nicholas Lane, Lewes, Sussex BN7 2JZ
pomegranatepress@aol.com   01273 470100
www.pomegranate-press.co.uk

Text © Jim Barham 2010
Registered with the UK Copyright Service UK©CS, registration no. 316630
Illustrations © Leanne Dodd
Front cover illustration courtesy of British Airways Heritage Centre

ISBN 978-1-907242-08-3

British Library Cataloguing-in-Publication Data.
A catalogue record for this book is available from the British Library

Printed by 4Edge. 7A Eldon Way, Hockley, Essex SS5 4AD

CONTENTS

ACKNOWLEDGEMENTS

My thanks to Judy Barham, Rowland and Marian Myers, Leanne Dodd, Carolyn Houston, Claire Barham, Paul Currell, Victor Marquis (the editor of St.Lucia's paper *The Voice)*, Ian Underdown, Paul Jarvis and Howell Green at the British Airways Heritage Centre, David Arscott at Pomegranate Press and Tony and Sheila Amin, who one night talked me into writing this book.

INTRODUCTION

I had always loved to travel, so in the summer of 1971 I applied to become an air steward with BOAC (British Overseas Airways Corporation). Some six weeks later I was invited to London for an interview and a group exercise. The selection process was thorough, and only 10 per cent of those who applied would be successful. So having done my best, I went home and kept my fingers crossed.

Towards the end of the year, I was summoned to London's Heathrow Airport for a medical. To all intents and purposes this was just a formality, but I had a rather obvious secret: at that time to be an air steward one could be no taller than 6ft 2ins, and I was 6ft 4ins. My heart was in my mouth when I entered the surgery to see the company doctor.

After I had stripped down to my underwear, we went through all the usual checks and I was given a gown to wear (the sort that you wear in hospital for an operation). This came down below my knees – and an idea suddenly came to me . . .

Just before the doctor checked my height, he said that he had to leave the room for a moment. I looked at the measure on the wall and noticed that it only went up to a maximum height of 6ft 2ins. Now was the time to initiate my cunning plan! I positioned myself against the measure, bent my knees and waited for the doctor's return. He picked up his clip board and announced, '6 feet 2 inches; just right!', adding, 'You can stand up straight now.'

I was in.

6ft 2

6ft 2" Just right you can stand up straight now!

I was to learn that as long as one arrived for one's flights on time and looked presentable, then the world awaited! I also soon discovered that I was working alongside some great characters. In common with other groups of workers who have to deal with the general public, the humour among airline crew was at times black and occasionally cruel. Within the ranks of the crew were former servicemen, nurses, policemen, merchant seamen, lawyers and graduates – in other words, people from all walks of life.

During my years in the airline I had great fun. I still miss the laughs and good times that I shared with my colleagues, and I thank them all for the memories, some of which I have included here.

"BRITISH OVERSEAS AIRWAYS CORPORATION

PMS OCR

Mr J P M Barham
14 Herne Hill
Mansions Herne Hill
London S E 24 9QN

4

20 January 1972

Dear Mr Barham

I have pleasure in confirming your engagement as a member of BOAC Air Cabin Crew. Please report to the Air Cabin Crew Training Centre, Cranebank at 0845 hours on Monday 21 February 1972.

When reporting to the Cabin Crew Training Centre, you must bring the following –
    P45 Income Tax Form
    National Insurance Card
  (a) Passport with not less than six months to expiry '
    Passport to contain a receat photograph
    Passport title officially changed to AIR STEWARD-
        or AIR STEWARDESS – no other title will be accepted/
    50p postal order for an Air Crew Member's certificate.

    FAILURE TO ACTION THE ABOVE REQUIREMENTS OR TO PRODUCE THESE DOCUMENTS ON THE DAY YOU REPORT MAY CAUSE YOUR TRAINING TO BE SOSTPONED.

The terms and conditions of your employment are set out in the accompanying Notice of Staff Engagement, which also shows details essential to your basic personal record, e.g. previous service with BOAC or BEA may carry with it certain entitlements. Please read and check the document, indicate your acceptance by signing the declaration on the reverse, and return immediately to me. The copy is for you to keep.

        Selection Services
        Administration Superintendent
        Ext. 3881

1/72

PO Box 10 · Hounslow · Middlesex   01-759 5511

CHAPTER 1

VC10 and 707 Fleet, aka 'Minis'

Before new entrant cabin crew were allowed near an aircraft or a passenger, they had to undergo a six-week induction training course, which was held at the training centre at Cranebank close to the airport (or as we called it, 'Braincrank'). This course covered the basics of good customer service, meal routines, cultural awareness and what was known as Safety Equipment and Emergency Procedures, or as we referred to it, SEP. The initial induction course was a pass or a fail, and from our course we lost a couple of aspiring cabin crew members.

However, the SEP course was where things really got serious. SEP covered basic medical training, fire fighting, deploying life rafts and inflating lifejackets at Heston swimming pool (great fun!), learning the exact position of all the safety equipment on the aircraft and practising evacuations – going down escape slides in the various mock-ups in Cranebank. The SEP part of the course left the instructors no room for discretion. If anyone failed the first time they were given one more chance, and if they still failed to attain the required legal standard, they were out.

After three weeks or so, we were taken to the uniform stores to be fitted for our uniforms. These were the domain of Mr Rafferty and his team. He was a colourful Irishman who oversaw all that went on in the stores, which at this time were known as Rafferty's Boutique.

The 'boutique' was located in the west of Heathrow airport, and consisted of a selection of Nissan huts with corrugated roofs. The stores supplied uniforms to all staff, male and female.

The uniform for men was of a military style: dark blue trousers and double breasted jacket, with rank markings on the jacket sleeves and on the epaulets of a white shirt. The captains' jackets were covered in gold, with four thick stripes on the sleeves, and the same on their epaulets, plus gold 'scrambled egg' on the peaks of their caps. Many of them had flown during the Second World War and proudly wore their medal ribbons on their jackets beneath their wings. They sparkled in the sunshine.

Junior 'boy' stewards, on the other hand, had one thin gold ring on their jacket sleeve and the same on the shirt epaulets. The gold stripe looked more like a laundry mark, and as a result the 'boys' had to rely on their personality and charm to be taken seriously. The stewards were also furnished with a cap, which was much hated as it made them look like station porters. The senior cabin crew were driven mad trying to enforce uniform standards that stated the hat should always be worn in public.

Uniform standards were strictly enforced and not subject to negotiation, and all cabin crew were inspected as they signed in for their flights.

Once all the various assessments had been passed we were given our first trips flying as extra crew. The rosters were read out, and we had trips going all over the BOAC network. Amazingly, there were some people from that course who I never saw again – showing what a big company we had joined. My supernumary trip was to Dubai, a place that I had never even heard of.

First Trip
My first flight was on a Boeing 707 aircraft. Dubai in the early 70s was a very different place compared with the modern city it has become in recent years. However, it was still exciting and it was also the first Arab state that I had ever visited.

The crew hotel overlooked the Creek from where the dhows travelled far and wide. This hotel was by today's standards very basic, providing guests with few facilities; however its unique selling point was that one could sit on the loo while having a shower, a feature that I have never found anywhere else in 40 years of travelling.

In those early days I was learning the ropes, keeping quiet and watching what went on, following the advice of a friend, which was, 'You have two ears and one mouth, so listen twice as much as you speak'.

Before I started flying, I had jobs with varying levels of responsibility and I thought that I was quite street-wise, with little more to learn. However, I was soon to realise that this was not the case . . .

Sticky Money

In those days alcoholic drinks were not complimentary in Economy class, so there was a charge for any drinks consumed during the flight. On my first operational flight to Dubai I was given the task of collecting the money for these drinks from the customers. Most people gave me notes in large denominations, which meant I was constantly walking back and forth to the rear galley to get change from the cash box.

At some stage the senior steward, a veteran of cruise ships, took me to one side and gave me a tip. He suggested that instead of returning the change to the customer on a silver gallery tray, I should take it out on a plastic tray. I replied that I had been told to use a gallery tray at the training centre, whereupon he smiled, took a plastic tray, wetted it and put a 50 pence piece onto it. He said, 'If you can pick this up, it's yours!' I tried very hard, but couldn't separate the coin from the tray's wet surface. I then discovered that neither could many of the passengers, who would often say after struggling to pick up the coins, 'Oh, keep the change'.

Flight deck visits

Until the terrorist attacks of 9/11, and only at the discretion of the captain, passengers were permitted, if accompanied by a crew member, to visit the flight deck. It was a great public relations exercise, as nine times out of ten dads would ask if their child could have a look. Once there, the dads were often more fascinated than the children.

Nervous flyers were nearly always more settled once they had visited the flight deck, having realised that the people flying the aircraft were reassuringly (in most cases) members of the human race.

All sorts of people went to meet the flight crew, and there were some funny incidents along the way, two of which follow.

WW2 Veteran

Inevitably on a long night flight there are those passengers who are unable to sleep. One night, such a person in the First Class cabin drifted towards the galley and started talking to me.

This particular gentleman was from Germany and had flown bombers for the Luftwaffe during the Second World War. After a while, he asked if he could visit the flight deck. I went forward and, after speaking to the captain, was told that I could bring him up. Introductions were made and the passenger told the flight crew about how he used to fly Heinkel bombers during the war. Everyone was interested in hearing what he had to say, and there were smiles all round.

Emboldened by the interest and hospitality shown thus far, he grew more confident, saying, 'Ah yes, I remember very well being at the controls of my Heinkel over Coventry – great days!'

The atmosphere on the flight deck suddenly became somewhat frosty and you could feel the tension rising. At this point, the first officer turned round in his seat and retorted, 'I believe if we beat you lot once more, we get to keep the cup!'

The passenger promptly left the flight deck, without another word.

Age of the Aircraft

On a visit to the flight deck of a VC10, a lady was being patiently talked through all the instruments, levers and switches. When the captain had finished his explanations, the lady asked him the age of the aircraft. He replied, '15'. The lady thought for a moment and then asked, 'Would you drive a 15-year-old car?', to which he responded, 'I would if it was powered by four Rolls Royce Conway engines!'

Curry in a Hurry

How often, have you found yourself thinking that some one else's job is so much more glamorous than your own? The following story demonstrates the old adage 'Where there's muck there's brass'.

This incident took place on a Boeing 707 which was approaching Heathrow Airport, having come from Bombay (Mumbai) via Dubai – it was some 15 minutes from landing. For most of the approach the seat belt sign had been illuminated as a result of the strong turbulence, making it hazardous to move around. The cuspidors (sick bags) were being filled as the aircraft lurched around the sky.

Those cabin crew who were responsible for the aircraft bars were counting the bar stocks and completing the customs paperwork before closing the bars for landing. The steward who was working in the rear section of the aircraft was busy counting one of the bars. The position of this unit meant that he was blocking the access to the rear toilets.

The steward heard a male passenger who was standing by him say, 'Please – I must use the toilet!' He pointed out that, as the aircraft was about to land, the gentleman should return to his seat. Again, the man said (this time more urgently), 'But I must use the toilet!' The steward looked up and repeated his previous instructions. He continued with his stock check, whereupon the passenger threw up – all over him! He must have previously been eating a curry, and the steward was now in the unfortunate position of wearing it!

The passenger immediately said, 'So sorry!' and quickly returned to his seat, leaving the crew to clean their colleague up as best they could just before the wheels of the aircraft touched down at LHR.

About an hour later, back at the airline's offices, the steward wondered why he was being given immediate access to the front of the queue of cabin crew waiting to pay in their bar monies. He soon realised that the extra politeness of his colleagues was purely down to the unpleasant odour emitting from his uniform.

Voyage Reports

To ensure continuity in customer service requirements on board the airline's fleet around the world, every long-haul aircraft contained among the documentation a record of the flight, called a Voyage Report. This report detailed any incidents, such as technical snags, delays and passenger information, and it was used by the next crew to update themselves after taking over at transit stops.

Most reports would read, rather mundanely, 'All passengers travelled well', and in order to complete the various paperwork required of the senior crew member, the V/R would often be completed before the end of the flight, when all seemed to be going according to plan.

However, there was one brief but infamous report, which read: 'All passengers travelled well – except for 15A, who died.'

Training Stewards

In the early days as a new entrant one was under fairly close scrutiny, and as well as written in-flight assessments carried out by the chief steward, a training steward would often appear at an outstation or on an incoming aircraft, his objective being to check the whole crew. Some of these training stewards had come from the Services and had been there, done it etc, and they seemed to have a very jaundiced view of us whipper-snappers. When they were on board the aircraft I was very wary of them, and as they had nicknames such as 'the Hat', 'Doctor Death', 'Mr Thick', 'El Cid', 'Cuff Hemmings' and 'Howling Green', I probably had just cause.

However, with the benefit of hindsight, I know that beneath their tough exterior they were empathic and caring people.

Promotion to First Class

After two or three years working in the Economy cabins, promotion came to those eligible crew who had successfully completed the first-class course. Working in First Class preparing the high quality meals and giving silver service was great fun, and it meant that we came into contact with a true variety of people, both famous and infamous. There were also those customers who both regarded and treated us like servants, but luckily they were few and far between.

There were seats for twenty-four First Class passengers on the 707, and twenty on the VC10. For this service there would be two cabin crew who, when the aircraft was full, were helped by the chief steward, who would float between the First Class and Economy cabins as required – although sometimes the 'chief' could be more of a hindrance than a help!

Every now and then the meal service did not quite go to plan . . .

First Class Lunch is served in the Economy Cabin

The stewardess and I took our seats for take off, as the aircraft lined up on the runway. Everything in the galley was secure – or so I thought. The aircraft started to roll, slowly gathering speed and then, at the appropriate moment, the nose lifted and we were airborne. From that moment, however, time stood still for me – in my last-minute checks I had somehow forgotten to secure the First Class fridge door!

As the aircraft climbed steeply, the inevitable happened. The door swung open, spilling all the contents of the fridge out onto the galley floor with a resounding crash! Still on my crew seat, there was nothing I could do but watch with horror, as the twenty First Class passengers saw their lunch head past them towards the rear of the aircraft, leaving a trail of gravy and ice cream on the cabin floor.

It must be said, however, that those unfortunate passengers were all very understanding: they were amused by my mistake and subsequent embarrassment. I have no doubt that they dined out on that story for quite a while afterwards.

French Lessons

The Pink Panther film had just been released, and Peter Sellers' portrayal of Inspector Clousseau was all the rage, with the French accent being copied by everyone. Cabin crew were no exception.

I don't know how it started, but I happened to be mimicking the phoney French accent one day when speaking to the passengers. The customers in First Class seemed to be amused by my ham-fisted performance, which unfortunately encouraged me and made me bolder.

The aircraft had stopped off at an outstation, and some joining passengers had boarded for the onward sector. My 'Clousseau is now a steward performance' continued unabated. I spoke to one of the joining First Class passengers, who happened to be French. Not only had he not seen the Pink Panther film, but he thought that I was French and immediately launched into deep conversation, for which my school boy French was ill prepared. He soon realised that I had not understood most of what he had said and I experienced that bad feeling that one gets when things start to go very wrong.

''Ow do you 'ave a French accent, yet you clearly do not understand me?' he ventured.

I replied, 'Well, my Muzer was French but my Fuzer was Engleesh – my parents never spoke to me in any uzer language but Engleesh, so the onlee ting zat I picked up from 'er, was 'er accent.'

The passenger smiled knowingly and said no more, but he clearly did not believe a word of my hastily thought up answer.

For the next six hours the Frenchman took every opportunity to engage me in conversation, asking questions about my family roots. I was forced to keep up the French accent, much to the amusement of my fellow crew members. I longed for the aircraft to land so that I could abandon the façade. Certainly I never again attempted to impersonate Inspector Clousseau!

Customs & Excise
I quickly learnt that the way to stay on the right side of any customs officer was to keep quiet, and only speak when spoken to.

The Customs and Excise in Birmingham had a reputation for being thorough. This was to be expected, as it was said that customs officers were trained in Birmingham.

In the early days when landing in the UK all crew were required to make a written customs declaration, which was generally sufficient. However, every now and then they would be 'rummaged'. This meant that all the crew suitcases and cabin bags would be searched, and if an officer had any reason to believe that one's declaration was false, there was nowhere that they could not search if they so desired.

On this particular day we had flown in from New York. I had not been flying long and I had bought about twenty record albums, which in those days were considerably cheaper than they would have been in the UK.

The officer came to me, looked at my declaration form and started to search my belongings.

'So have you any more LPs that you have not yet told me about?' he asked. I was relaxed as I had nothing to hide, but somehow the mischievous side of me seemed to take over! I thought for a moment and then replied, 'Oh yes, I forgot to mention the other five that I have secreted up my backside!'

Time stood still, while the customs officer looked at me quizzically, before calmly stating, 'I will give you one more chance to answer my question, otherwise you will be searched, and if we do not find anything, you will be prosecuted for making a false declaration.'

I realised that I had gone too far, and from that moment on, I was never anything but straight with customs officers.

After arriving at the hotel, it was customary for all the crew to gather in one of the crew rooms for a night cap and a natter. This would normally be in the largest room, which more often than not belonged to the most senior crew member or the captain. Usually the cabin crew and flight crew stayed at the same hotels.

On this occasion, after our arrival at the hotel, we checked in and were allocated our various rooms. The captain said that he was feeling tired and was going to go straight to bed. However, he agreed to swap his room with anyone who wanted to host the room party. I volunteered to swap my room with him, so we exchanged our room keys. Then we all went to our rooms to wait for our suitcases to be brought up by the hotel porters.

There was a knock at my door, and there outside stood the porter with my case. He followed me into the room and asked, 'Where should I put your bag, captain?' I told him that I was not the captain, as we had exchanged rooms. He looked at me in total amazement, before responding, 'But all the Engleesh captains have parties! Is he not Engleesh?'

So, having had your night cap, and by now feeling totally exhausted, it was time for undisturbed sleep. Oh, but if life were so simple!

The Crew Disturbance Unit

It would seem that the more tired you were, the greater the chance that you would suffer from noise caused by the dreaded crew disturbance unit, otherwise known as hotel maintenance workers. This odious group operated world wide, and their ability to make noise was unparalleled. As well as operations within the hotel, generally either above, below or next door to our rooms, they also operated within the grounds of the hotel.

Complaints to the hotel reception desk were futile, as this resourceful group were above the law. I can think of no place in the world where I have not suffered at the hands of this successful international franchise.

It would seem that I was not the only one to suffer, as the following story demonstrates.

Room Service with a difference!

The flight to Calcutta had been long and arduous, and the stewardess had settled into her room, looking forward to some well-earned rest. She fell asleep almost at once.

Some time after that a low, soft, swishing sound came in to her dreams, and this noise eventually woke her up. Still groggy with tiredness, she tried to work out what it could be, as it was becoming quite disconcerting. She realised that it was actually coming from within her hotel bedroom,

which was blacked out with thick curtains. She didn't dare move. Finally, not being able to bear the tension any longer, she reached for the bedside light switch. At that moment, from above her head came a voice saying, 'Do not worry, madam . . . just painting the ceiling!'

Turning on the light, she found that there was indeed a decorator in her room, standing on his ladder with brush in one hand and a paint pot in the other. Relieved that she was probably not in the company of a murderer, the stewardess, in so many words, asked him if he would leave her room and continue his decorating at a later date – an extreme example of the crew disturbance unit at work!

Ditching Drills

As has been previously mentioned, a thorough knowledge of the emergency drills was required, and every year the crew were called in for their annual refresher, which covered all the drills and locations of emergency equipment. In the exam anything less than 99% was unacceptable. So as you can imagine, we took every chance to keep the procedures fresh in our minds. However, perhaps the next tale demonstrates a rather over zealous attention to duty.

In Colombo (now Sri Lanka) the crew used to stay in the same hotel as the RAF crews. In the reception area of the hotel, standing in pride of place on a pedestal, was a scaled down replica model of a Super VC10 aircraft.

Needless to say, when the two crews got together there were some epic evenings. Towards the end of the proceedings those with extra staying power would make their way over to the hotel pool, often with the scale model of the aircraft, in order to replicate the emergency ditching drills from the diving board. Much laughter would ensue, as the model would invariably sink.

Once the drills had been completed, the model would be returned to its stand to dry out once more!

The last that I heard of the model VC10 was that the RAF crew had removed the wings and super-glued them back to front on to the blighted model.

Then there were those crew members who were more interested in topping up their tans than hanging around in hotel bars . . .

Too splashy!

I had never been to Barbados, or anywhere else in the Caribbean for that matter, and I still vividly remember my first trip there.

The morning after our arrival at the beachside hotel I met up with other members of my crew on the beach and joined in with the general conversation and chatter. At some stage it was noticed that one of the stewardesses was missing. When away from home, cabin crew tended to move around collectively, much like a family, and as there were only six people on the crew one person missing would be noticed. Remarks were made, such as 'She wasn't in her room when I called her earlier', and 'I'm sure there's no problem – she's probably doing her own thing.'

I decided to have a walk and explore the grounds of the hotel. As I approached the hotel pool area I saw the missing stewardess covered in sun-tan lotion, doing some serious sunbathing. I wandered up and said cheerily, 'Hello'.

The girl opened an eye and returned my greeting, while smiling with a pained expression on her face. My presence was clearly not appreciated. Ignoring these signs, I pressed on,

'So why aren't you on the beach with rest of the crew?' I asked.

'I don't like the sea,' she replied.

'Why not?'

The girl removed her sunglasses with a sigh, glared at me and said, 'I hate the sea, because it splashes!' – after which, she put her sunglasses back on and closed her eyes. I took this as a sign that the conversation was over.

I slunk off, to join the rest of the crew back on the beach.

Having given up trying to sleep, keeping away from the splashy sea, and floating models of aircraft in the pool, it was time to venture outside the hotel and see what was going on, with the inevitable quality control checks in the local hostelries . . .

Down Under

Our crew had a day off in Melbourne and everyone had dispersed. I had arranged to have lunch with one of the other stewards. As can often happen, one beer led to another and it was way past lunchtime and not a morsel of food had passed our lips.

I ordered another round of cold beers from the barman, who summoned me closer in a conspiratorial fashion.

'Aren't you going to eat anything, mate?'

'There's a steak in every glass,' I replied knowingly.

He looked back at me in a very disapproving way, sniffed and said, 'If you don't eat, you don't sh–t and if you don't sh–t, you die!'

The Bard himself could not have put it better!

And so for the next nine years I remained on the Mini Fleet. The 707 and VC10 were single-aisle aircraft, with six cabin crew, two pilots and a flight engineer. Until the early 80s many of the older captains had flown operationally in the Second World War, and they were great characters with amazing stories to tell. As they retired, they were replaced by younger captains, many of whom were in their early thirties, so the fleet was operated by young crews who all knew each other.

We all recoiled at the thought of being one of fourteen or more crew on a Boeing 747 (known as 'Fat Albert'), but nothing lasts for ever, and the 707/VC10 Fleet was slowly wound down as crew were transferred to the 747 Fleet or the Lockheed Tristar. Consequently, the routes got fewer as the fleet became smaller, and then one day I received a roster to operate the last ever commercial flight of the VC10.

On the 29th March 1981 the last VC10 flight (registration GASGF) took place, commencing in Dar-es-Salaam, and stopping at Kilimanjaro and Larnaca before terminating at London Heathrow.

Before our take off from 'Dar', the captain got permission to make a spectacular low pass over the hotel where we had been staying. As the aircraft approached the hotel fast and low, it was obvious to see that the beach was packed with people waving their towels. From the ground, that fly-past was an awesome and moving site. It was rumoured that many of the fixed beach fittings ended up in the sea, succumbing to the engine draft as full power was selected and the aircraft climbed away.

There was a crew change in Larnaca. After it had taken off, the aircraft flew over Larnaca town and then came back to the airfield, flying past fast and low waggling its wings before climbing away with its four Conways making their distinguishable crackle.

Every one of us was in tears. It was a sad and dramatic sight, and I shall never forget it. An era had ended.

Engineer's Last Flight

It had been the flight engineer's last trip after 25 years of service before retirement. After landing, and before disembarking in Larnaca, I found him standing looking thoughtfully into the First Class toilet.

'Are you Ok?' I asked.

'Yes,' he replied, 'I was just looking at my handiwork.'

'What's that?' I asked.

'Well, I'm the person responsible for that notice in the toilet,' he said, pointing towards a small plaque on the wall.

It read, *Please close lid before flushing.*

'Every man has his moment of fame,' he said. 'And that was mine.'

Super VC10, GASGF. Dar-es-Salaam, 28th March 1981.

CHAPTER 2

Russian Visa

During the time that I flew on the Boeing 707 there was a requirement for volunteers to man the Polar and Siberian routes. For this all the crew needed to hold Russian visas.

The Boeing 707 made its first commercial flight for BOAC from London to New York on May 27th, 1960. The aircraft offered speed, comfort and value, and gave the general public access to long-haul flying.

May 5th 1969 saw the start of the 707 on the Polar route, and cut down the flying time between London and Tokyo when compared with the traditional route via the Middle East and India.

The sector from Moscow to Tokyo routed the aircraft over the Russian tundra, and if anyone cared to look out of the aircraft window there was little sign of life. However, if the aircraft went off track or changed altitude without clearance, a curt reminder to get back on track would come over the radio from a Russian air traffic controller somewhere below the aircraft.

The routing charts for the transit across Russia had little detail – only the latitude and longitude, and a line showing the airway running from east to west. The flight was overnight, and on occasions the outside temperature could get so low that aircraft would have to descend, as the fuel would become thick and in danger of freezing. Even with the heat turned up, the temperature in the cabin could get quite chilly. For the cabin crew, the night would be spent giving the passengers more blankets and hot drinks to keep them warm!

Anchorage

The flight from London to Anchorage would route north over the North Pole. In the 1970s Anchorage had the feel of a wild frontier town. At the time the Trans Alaskan pipeline was being installed, so the place was full of workers who used Anchorage for R & R. At night it was wild and had the feeling of a boom town (which it was).

At all times of the day and night there were lots of drunk Eskimos staggering around – mix these with the pipeline workers, light blue touch paper and stand well back.

In the winter there was little daylight, but this deprivation was rewarded with spectacular views of the Northern Lights. In summer it never really got dark. However, the downside were the industrial sized midges, which bit ferociously.

Rent a wreck

For the more intrepid crew, there was a great trip by road to Alyeska using the local car hire company called 'Rent a Wreck'. Unlike most car hire establishments this one insisted that the vehicle was returned with a scratch!

Example of a 'Rent a Wreck' vehicle.

Moscow

The crew hotel in Moscow, when lit, resembled a building from a Dracula film. The lobby was always busy and was populated with people from the Eastern Bloc. These people were visiting Moscow as part of trade delegations and cultural exchanges.

This hotel was vast, and there was even a doctor present, together with his/her own surgery. Each floor was laid with wooden parquet flooring, and had the building ever caught fire the hotel guests would have stood little chance of escape, as the doors to the stairwells always appeared to be locked.

Sitting behind a large solid desk on each floor, was a Dragon Lady (as she was affectionately known), who was responsible for her particular floor. The hotel lifts seemed very old and unreliable, so to use the emergency stairwell involved 'sweet talking' the Dragon Lady to get her to unlock the emergency exit doors. These rather stern ladies were also known to enjoy a tipple or two, which often succeeded in melting their rather tough exteriors. Occasionally they were spotted taking a sip from a hidden bottle (usually vodka) kept out of sight beneath their desks, which doubtless helped to relieve the boredom of sitting in an empty hotel corridor all day.

As is usual in most hotels, each room had a telephone. However, what was not so usual was that these phones would ring ominously at all times of the day and night. On answering the telephone, there never appeared to be anyone at the other end, which only added to our frustration and annoyance! The calls were doubtless made by the Russian franchise of the odious Crew Disturbance Unit. Speaking in whispers, we would exchange tales with our colleagues and fantasise about these odd telephone calls, imagining all sorts of skulduggery associated with the Cold War. We heard (probably wrongly) that the rooms contained bugging devices which were monitored by the KGB. If there were such devices in the hotel rooms, little would have been learned in the way of secrets from our crews.

The weather could bring staggeringly cold temperatures during the long winter months, but that did not deter these tough and resilient Muscovites.

One freezing night the aircraft had a technical problem, and to fix it the ground engineers had to work outside with no protection. The passengers disembarked while the crew remained on board. It was so cold in the cabin that the only way to keep warm was to sit in the centre of the aircraft covered with blankets.

While working on the troublesome engine, the engineers took it in turns to board the aircraft to warm up. To warm their hands they would put them in the ice buckets! It took three hours to fix the engine. All the while the Russian border guards stood rigidly to attention by the aircraft doors. In spite of our entreaties, they would not accept any hot drinks. They wore only their uniform covered by a great coat, with long boots, gloves and a cap.

On every flight arrival and once the doors were opened, the Russian border guards would position themselves by the doors at each end of the aircraft to check that no unauthorised person boarded the aircraft during the stop-over. These men would always be the first people we would see when opening the aircraft doors on arrival at Moscow, and they would usually greet us with a cursory nod.

To make my life more interesting during my trips over there I began to learn a bit of Russian conversation, and on one overnight flight from Tokyo to Moscow I learned how to say 'Hello, sailor!' in Russian. After landing in Moscow, the aircraft door swung open revealing the usual burly member of the border guard. Encouraged by my colleagues, I let rip with great confidence and announced, in my best Russian, 'Hello, sailor!' to the unwary soldier. He froze and held me in his icy stare. 'You have gone too far, this time,' I thought. The uneasy silence was broken by a member of the ground staff who spoke to the soldier. I do not know what he said to the guard, but he told me that I had been very fortunate and had had a lucky escape. The border guard was not amused.

In the early 70s buying a meal in Moscow was a bit hit and miss, so airline crews took away any unused catering from the aircraft to the hotel. On every other floor in the hotel there were buffets/cafes where ladies would heat our meals for us and produce fresh omelettes. The only snag with this arrangement was that these buffets/cafes would often close at lunchtime, making it quite a challenge to find anything to eat.

Now and then we would go down to the main restaurant in the hotel, but even though it was quite expensive, it was popular with the locals and visitors and was nearly always fully booked! The food produced there was typical Russian fare, and the chicken Kiev and the borscht (beetroot soup) were particularly good.

Christmas Day Party
This particular Christmas the trip left the UK on 20th December. The first

sector was to Anchorage in Alaska, with some time off for us there, followed by 24 hours off in Tokyo, from where we departed on Christmas Eve, arriving in Moscow on Christmas Day.

Before leaving home, all the crew were informed that they had been invited to the British embassy's Christmas Day party in Moscow, hosted by the British ambassador and his wife. We were all told to pack suitable attire (lounge suits for the men and smart dresses for the ladies).

We landed at Moscow about lunch time and after a short rest (having flown the long sector from Tokyo), we all met in the hotel lobby 'booted and suited'. We were duly collected by an embassy vehicle and, after passing the Russian guard at the entrance, we entered the embassy grounds.

The party was split into two areas. In one room there was pop music playing and the majority of the people in there were students who were studying in Moscow.

Standing in amongst the students, our crew stood out like sore thumbs in our smart clothes. We started to feel quite awkward, when a very elegant lady (the ambassador's wife) came up to us.

'Are you the BA crew?' she asked.

'Yes,' we replied.

'Then come with me,' she said, walking through a doorway and into another much larger room.

Judging by the noise of conversation and laughter emanating from the doorway, this room was obviously the hub of the party, as it was filled with embassy staff including various military attaches, men in grey suits (security officers), section heads, secretaries, business men and wives and friends of the embassy staff.

We were welcomed warmly into the group and spent a fascinating evening learning about the lives of the embassy staff in Moscow, who lived and worked with the knowledge that most of what they said and did was constantly being monitored. We had a great evening with them all, dancing till dawn, with the ambassador leading the way.

Some months later, the prime minister visited Moscow, and in the television coverage I saw the ambassador standing at the bottom of the aircraft steps with his team. It made me wonder if the prime minister had had as good a night as we had enjoyed – maybe not.

Tokyo

Tokyo was a fascinating place, as it was so totally different from other parts of the world, in terms of the language, food, culture, everything! In the 70s the Japanese were generally not as tall as most westerners, and I can still clearly remember my first trip on the metro, as it wasn't built with people of my height in mind. The hand-holds for those who were standing only came up to my shoulders. Anyone over 6ft tall was regarded with great interest, to the point of amusement. The schoolgirls thought us hilarious, covering their mouths and sniggering as we struggled in vain to make ourselves a little less conspicuous on the crowded metro!

I remember a Japanese child in the Ginza district standing transfixed while looking at me from my toes up, finally tipping his head back as far as it would go inorder to take in my full height, with his mouth dropping wide open in astonishment. His poor mother was deeply embarrassed by his reaction!

Leanne 200

The crew hotel in Tokyo was the Tokyo Prince, which was a few stops on the metro from the Ginza shopping area. It was said that it was built on the site of a Samurai graveyard, and in the lobby, in a glass case, was a statue of a full-sized model of a Samurai. This added to the myth that the hotel was haunted!

Say it again

The nearest train station to the hotel was called Onarimon, which is where I went on this particular day to buy my train ticket. In those days not many Japanese spoke English, and I struggled to make myself understood. The more I repeated the station's name, the more the ticket clerk looked back at me with astonishment.

Luckily we were all saved further embarrassment by a very helpful English speaking Japanese man, who very kindly came to our rescue – although to my ear his pronunciation of Onarimon wasn't much different to mine!

'Automatic' Tickets
In common with most railway stations worldwide, travellers in Tokyo can buy their train tickets at automatic vending machines.

One day I was in a queue at one of these machines when I noticed that the man in front of me was becoming very agitated. It was clear to me that he was angry, having put his money in the machine without a ticket being produced. He finally lost his temper and began to hit the machine while also kicking it very hard. The next moment, the door on the front of the ticket machine swung open – to reveal a station employee who, from inside the machine handed a ticket to the astonished passenger before promptly slamming the door shut again!

As the 707 Fleet became smaller, these trips over the Pole to Anchorage, Tokyo and Moscow became fewer and were gradually taken over by the newer and much larger 747 aircraft, which heralded the end of yet another era in airline travel.

On May 24th 1982, almost 22 years to the day since the 707 had entered service with BOAC, the aircraft – now in British Airways livery – made its last commercial flight from Cairo to London.

BOAC Boeing 707 being refuelled in Anchorage, Alaska. [British Airways Heritage Centre]

CHAPTER 3

Boeing 747s

After the VC10 fleet was disbanded, the cabin crew who had not already transferred to other fleets were left with a reduced route network on the 707. Consequently they were offered the options of transferring to 747s, Tristars or Concorde fleets.

I opted for 747s, as it was financially better due to the fact that the fleet had a greater and more varied route network at that time. However, from the minute that I started the conversion course I felt that I had made a mistake. This was not helped by seeing lots of chums from the old fleet who had opted to go to the Tristar fleet (more of that later). Gone were the days of a small close-knit community, and the thought of being part of a cabin crew team of fourteen or more made me cringe. Having said that, I found everyone was very welcoming and kind.

Often on a three-day trip it was possible never to speak to the crew working at the other end of the aircraft, and the crew would often split up once on the ground and socialise only with the colleagues with whom they had been working. When all the crew and flight deck crew did go out to eat en masse, it was often a bun fight. Imagine trying to serve food to seventeen people at the same time: it was a nightmare, and when the bill appeared the fun really started as we tried to work out who had eaten what!

Raining sauce
It was my first trip on the 747 aircraft since being transferred from the 707/VC10 Fleet and I was working in the Upper Deck, which was configured as a First Class cabin.

As the passenger loads were light that day, my first flight was relatively easy, leaving me time to settle in to the new routines and familiarise myself with the aircraft's systems.

Eventually, with about 45 minutes left before landing, I began to start cleaning up in the galley, throwing away any unused liquids and foodstuff into the rubbish bin. We were twenty minutes into the descent when the chief steward came bounding up the stairs from the First Class cabin on the main deck. He was in a state of panic, as apparently since the start of the descent a brown sludge like liquid had been seeping through the cabin ceiling and depositing itself on the unfortunate First Class passengers sitting underneath.

The flight engineer came down from the flight deck, as he was worried that the aircraft was leaking hydraulic fluid – a potentially dangerous situation. He reached up to the cabin ceiling, touched the brown liquid with his finger and tasted it – declaring that it was *not* hydraulic fluid before returning to the flight deck to prepare for landing, which was by now imminent.

After landing, and fortunately once the cleaners had cleaned up the cabin floor and ceiling, questions were asked in an effort to establish the cause of the problem. While I was giving my account of things, which as far as I was concerned had no bearing on the situation, the chief steward said to me, 'You didn't put any unused food or liquid into the rubbish bin in your upper deck galley did you, because that bin is only suitable for dry waste?'

I innocently responded that on the aircraft conversion course no one had told me that fact, but in any case, I would never do anything so stupid.

That, luckily, was the end of the matter, but until that aircraft went in for its major service, residuals of my guilty secret continued to drip from the ceiling whenever the aircraft was landing.

Fifty Ways
Prior to showing passengers the safety briefing on the aircraft it was the duty of the senior crew member to somehow persuade the passengers to watch and familiarise themselves with the emergency exits, escape routes and safety equipment.

Unfortunately, however much they were cajoled and encouraged to pay attention to the demonstration, many passengers would often continue to read, talk or sleep through it.

In an effort to persuade his customers to pay attention to this important demonstration, a colleague of mine came up with this announcement: 'Ladies and gentlemen, there may be fifty ways to leave your lover, but there are only eight exits on this aircraft, so your attention to the following safety briefing would be appreciated.'

The airline had many fun characters who were great to fly with, as they were a constant source of amusement to the rest of the crew.

Don
The meal service on the 747 had been completed – drinks, lunch, coffee and liqueurs had all been served and the cabin crew had now turned their attention to eating their crew meals and having a well deserved cup of tea.

One of the crew, called Don, fell into his seat, took a deep breath and started to eat his meal. At this point, an American passenger approached and looked down at him, saying, 'Any chance of a Coke?'

Now, rightly or wrongly, Don felt that this was an intrusion and replied abruptly, 'Why don't you ---- off!'

The American was struck dumb. He was furious (and who can blame him?) The senior crew member was sent for, and all three went forward to the front of the aircraft to sort out a very difficult situation. After twenty minutes all sides of the story had been heard, with Don sticking to his guns and denying vigorously that he would ever say such a thing to a passenger. The senior crew member summed up by saying that he agreed that a crew member (especially one with Don's experience) would never swear in front of a customer.

The American gentleman relented and pointed out that as he had been travelling for nearly 24 hours, he must have misheard Don's response. All parties then shook hands, the American went back to his seat. Don returned to his by now cold crew meal, and calm returned once more to the aircraft.

Now that harmony and bonhomie reigned again, the American returned to the galley, where Don was about to eat his reheated meal.

'So Don, any chance I can get that Coke now?'

The inevitable followed: 'I thought I told you to ---- off!'

The bemused passenger returned to his seat once more, shaking his head.

Arthur

The next two stories are about Arthur, one of the airline's great characters – he was very talented and flamboyant with a rapier sharp wit.

On this occasion, the First Class passengers were boarding the aircraft with the usual pomp and ceremony that accompanied such occasions, with coats, jackets and hats being taken by the crew to be hung in the wardrobe or put in the overhead lockers.

Among the melée, a lady called to Arthur, who was the senior crew member, abruptly demanding that he should take her mink coat and hang it in the wardrobe. In the flash of an eye he replied, 'Madam, I would like to help, but I am allergic to nylon!'

The lady's reaction is not known.

In another incident, Arthur was getting out of a taxi in New York. He paid the driver and was walking away from the cab, when the driver called to him out of the window to tell him that he had left his umbrella behind, shouting 'Hey, fairy! You forgot your wand!'

On taking the umbrella from the driver, Arthur pointed it at him, saying, 'Turn to sh.t!'

Err or Err?

On long haul flights, once the aircraft was airborne, passengers were generally served a hot meal with drinks from the bar, followed by afternoon tea or a light snack prior to arrival at the destination. So it was quite possible during a flight on a fully loaded 747 to pour hundreds of cups of tea and coffee. More often than not, the question 'Tea or coffee?' was met with a blank stare, at which point it became necessary to go through one's repertoire of how to say tea or coffee in twenty different languages (a party piece that can be quite entertaining). A round of hot drinks could therefore often take some time.

It had been such a day, and the crew had the devil in them! Some wag suggested that instead of the usual question 'Tea or coffee?' we should just offer 'Err or err?' to see what the passengers' reaction would be. We all vowed that we would stick to the plan, and out we went, armed with our tea and coffee pots.

The result was that very few of the passengers asked us to repeat ourselves or even queried what we were saying. In fact it is true to say that the hot drinks service went faster than usual! However, when we repeated the exercise for top-ups, the passengers were getting into the swing of things, and they started asking us for a cup of 'err' – proving yet again that it is not what you say, but the way that you say it.

Chicken or Beef?

When serving a hot lunch or dinner to passengers, invariably the choice for the main course was for either chicken or beef. As repeating the question 'Would you like the chicken or beef option' became a little repetitive for 200–300 people, the crew would sometimes revert to 'Would you prefer feather or leather?', which would sometimes raise a smile or two.

Nairobi

There always seemed to be someone who got involved in daft situations and incidents, and life on 747s when off duty overseas was no different.

I had been waiting for over thirty minutes since my order for breakfast had been given to the waiter. A pot of tea had come at once, along with some rather soggy toast, but there was no sign of the rest of my order. As the waiter passed me, I enquired pleasantly when my meal might be arriving.

'It's coming,' he replied rather too quickly.

'And so is Christmas, but which will be here sooner?' I asked again.

The waiter pulled himself up to his full height and looking me in the eye he remarked, 'Christmas!'

Shortly after that the cooked breakfast arrived, accompanied with much more banter and humour from the cheeky waiter.

Delsey Dining

If the hotel restaurants did not appeal there was always an alternative. As the hotel meal allowances were such an integral part of the pay package, there were times when individuals, for various reasons, preferred to take the majority of their allowance home with them, rather than spending it while they were away. This led to the practice known as 'Delsey Dining', so named because at the time most crew used Delsey suitcases.

The crew would bring food, hot cups (small mugs like plug-in kettles) and dip-sticks (also used to boil water inside a mug or other receptacle). The joke was that when all the various appliances were plugged into the hotel light sockets/wall plugs and switched on, all the lights and television sets in the hotel would dim and flicker.

I was on a 14-day trip to the Far East, when I came into contact with a pair of stewards who were past masters in the art of Delsey Dining!

These two were enjoying some breakfast in the hotel in Singapore when I joined them. I don't remember how the subject came up, but I guess that we were discussing our next destination, which was to be Muscat (in the Gulf States) where the allowances were known to be very good, due to the high cost of living.

We were due to have 48 hours off in Muscat, and these two characters mentioned their catering plans. Sensing my interest, they offered to include me, and suggested that if I was interested in joining them my share of the costs would be £20. I took them up on their offer, not sure what to expect.

To this day I don't know how on earth these two lads managed to produce food of such quality – they would certainly put any of the current TV chefs to shame, and they may well be running their own restaurants by now!

A Cruise in Bermuda

For the unwary crew member abroad, even a quiet lunch time drink could take an unexpected turn.

Bermuda was a popular place to visit and the crew hotel was located in St Georges, a pretty little town with nice local restaurants and bars, overlooking the water. From time to time, a cruise ship would stop there and disgorge its passengers. Very often, crew members from the cruise ships would also come ashore for a few hours of relaxation.

One particular evening some of the airline crew were in a bar in St Georges and they began a conversation with some of the crew from a visiting cruise liner. As the evening progressed, the various crew members disappeared off back to their hotel or ship, finally leaving just one BA crew member and two of the crew from the liner. As the bar was closing, the ship's crew asked the BA chap if he would like to come on board their ship and visit the crew bar, known affectionately as 'the Pig and Whistle'. He accepted their invitation, and off they went for a nightcap or two.

One thing led to another, and eventually all three men were feeling no pain, but as it was now very late the BA chap was offered a bed for the night on board the ship. Feeling a bit worse for wear, he gratefully accepted.

The following morning the hung-over crew member awoke to the noise of the ship's engines and the gentle rocking of the Atlantic Ocean. Suddenly wide awake, he realised that he had a serious problem – he thought that the ship's crew had forgotten all about him when they had put to sea! He vaguely remembered being told that the ship had sailed in from New York, and as he looked out of his cabin porthole he saw Bermuda disappearing into the distance, with New York getting closer.

In an instant his hangover disappeared, as he remembered that he was meant to be operating back to London that night on the aircraft, with pick-up at 2000 from the hotel. He promptly left the cabin where he had been sleeping, desperate to find anyone to whom he could explain his predicament, as he truly believed that he was now heading for New York with no means of identification.

Luckily he came face to face with one of the crew he had met the previous evening in St Georges, who said 'Hi, how are you feeling today? You certainly were on good form last night!'

Amazed at such flippancy, the BA crew member told the ship's crew of his probable impending arrest on arrival at New York and that if he missed the pick-up for his flight back to London, he would almost certainly lose his job.

'We're not going to New York. We're just going out to sea to clear the shore; then we're heading back in towards Hamilton [the capital of Bermuda]. When we arrive, we'll call a taxi to take you back to your hotel. You should be back by 1700, so no problem!'

There may have been no problem, but certainly a lesson was learned that night of the perils of boarding an ocean-going vessel after consuming a little too much alcohol.

Riot in Chicago

Even an innocent visit to the shops could take a twist as I was to find out. It was between Christmas and New Year, and I happened to be in Chicago, with 48 hours off before returning to London. The post Christmas sales were in full swing, and as I needed to buy some new bed linen I went out bright and early in search of some serious bargains.

The main shopping area was a bit of a walk from the hotel and it was a bitterly cold day, with a keen wind whistling down the streets – Chicago was certainly living up to its name of 'the windy city'. I wrapped up well and headed in the direction of the shops. As I came closer to the town centre I noticed large crowds of people all milling around the place and speaking in a language that I could not understand. However, I had only one thing on my mind – linen bargains – so I passed by with no more than a cursory glance over my shoulder. This turned out to be a mistake, as I was soon to discover.

Some time later in the morning I had made my purchases and stocked up on sheets and towels. Fortified with a mug of hot frothy coffee and a huge American style breakfast, I headed back in the direction of the hotel. As I pressed on, the crowds of people around me became dense and I realised that they were not shoppers. I then noticed that they were carrying banners in support of the newly formed Solidarity group led by the Polish shipyard worker Lech Walesa. Everyone seemed very friendly and there was no sign of trouble, but I had definitely been caught up in some sort of demonstration. It now dawned on me – the crowd that I had seen earlier on, must have been the demonstrators planning their march.

From the centre of this press of people I suddenly emerged with no one else in front of me except the Chicago police. I moved forward with the intention of passing through the policemen, only to be informed that this was not possible. I then tried to leave the demonstration from the side, but again I was stopped. I tried to point out to the most senior policeman that I was not part of the demonstration but a shopper returning to my hotel, hence the bags that I was carrying. I showed him my airline ID and passport, but my appeals were met with an icy stare and I was ordered abruptly to 'Get back in line!'

If you can't beat them, join them, I thought.

Then started the Polish protestors' 'walking guide' to all the prominent government buildings and embassies of Chicago, eventually culminating in the throwing of paint (with much gusto) at the Russian delegation.

Hours later, when I finally reached my hotel (still carrying my purchases) I was feeling more than a little weary and cold. I received several calls from colleagues who were concerned because they hadn't been able to contact me. I don't think anyone believed my story except for one stewardess, who said that she was astonished to see some Polish demonstrators on the lunchtime television news, with me on camera heading the demonstration, laden down with my bags of shopping!

Call-Time
To ensure that airline crew didn't miss their pick-up from the hotel to the airport, a wake-up call was always pre-arranged for one hour before the pick-up time. This system worked well in the main. However, in the event of a delay, the ground staff at the airport would call the hotel to let them know.

The Crew Disturbance Unit @ work!

If a delay to the pick-up was in the early hours, the hotel staff (if they were switched on) would automatically roll the call-time forward. There were, however, many cases of a call-time being rolled from, for example, 0200 to 0500. On receipt of this information the hotel reception would call the sleeping crew members at 0200, waking them up in order to inform them that the pick-up time (and therefore the call-time) had been delayed until 0500!

This usually successfully resulted in none of the crew getting any more sleep for the rest of the night – another example of the Crew Disturbance Unit at work.

CHAPTER 4

Tristar and Short-Haul Flying

The Lockheed Tristar Fleet, was known by the cabin crew as the 'No Jacket Required' Fleet, as the male crew members seemed unable (or unwilling) to wear their in flight jackets during the meal service. At this time, the album 'No Jacket Required' had been released by Phil Collins, and the name was affectionately adopted by the Tristar crews.

Initially the Tristar predominantly flew to the Gulf (Saudi Arabia, Emirates, and Bahrain). The majority of the passengers were oil workers, and whether going to or from their destination, they generally enjoyed a drink or two. For those who worked in Saudi Arabia alcohol was not available, but for some of those who lived in compounds owned by their companies there was 'moonshine' and home brew available.

From a crew's perspective, the night flights back from the Gulf to London were unbelievable, as all most of the passengers wanted to do was to drink as much alcohol as possible. It was easier for us to give them triple measures, as a single didn't touch the sides. Then there was the rush towards the toilets at the rear of the aircraft, where the men would congregate, drinking and smoking. That area became known as Penny Lane.

As it was not permissible to smoke whilst standing up or moving around the cabin, there would be arguments when these passengers were told by the crew to either stop smoking or sit down. Two hours or so into the flight there were usually a few who would become intoxicated, so we would stop serving them drinks. After some protesting they would totter back to their seats and then fall asleep until the aircraft arrived at Heathrow. Some of them would look really rough when they disembarked, and the reactions of those nearest and dearest to them when they got home can only be imagined.

Those who worked in Saudi and in the Gulf had tough jobs and could not really be blamed for 'going for it' once on the aircraft. They were, generally speaking, a harmless lot and always apologised once they had slept off the alcohol, just in case they had upset anyone during the flight.

Sanctuary

Beneath the passenger cabins on the Tristar was the under-floor galley (or UFG). This area was manned by one crew member and was one of the more popular places to work on the aircraft, mainly because the crew member did not have to talk to the passengers. It was also used by the crew as a place to dry out clothes and swim wear that was still wet from the beach. From its depths came trolleys with hot food and duty free bars, as well as back-up catering supplies.

The area was surprisingly large, and on the starboard side forward of the wing there was a window from which the UFG steward/stewardess could survey the passing scenery while reading a newspaper or book during the odd quiet moment.

Items that were too big for the overhead hat racks were kept in the UFG – for example, children's pushchairs and large bags or packages.

You would think that nothing could go wrong keeping items of baggage in the UFG . . .

It's a Puzzle to Me

On this particular occasion, the Tristar was returning from yet another trip to Paris, carrying the usual 'chic' crowd. On boarding, a very smart looking lady demanded that someone should look after her 'very expensive' baby walker. The crew member who took it assured her that all would be well and not to worry. The lady shot him a look that said, 'There'll be trouble if it's damaged!' The baby walker was duly sent down in the lift to the UFG, in order to be 'safely' stowed for the flight back to Heathrow.

Prior to landing, it was custom and practice to load the push chairs in the UFG lift. Once the aircraft had landed and was taxiing to the stand, the lift was sent up to the cabin level. Now, once this lift was activated it would proceed on its way no matter what – nothing could stop the ascent. As the result of a heavy landing, the numerous baby walkers in the lift must have shifted, causing some sickening and expensive noises to come from its contents as the lift ascended.

Of course, it was inevitable that the baby walker that had come off worst happened to be the 'very expensive' model. It now looked like one of those metal puzzles that used to be present in Christmas stockings many years ago.

Meanwhile the unfortunate steward who had promised that no ill would befall the pushchair was feverishly trying to return it to some sort of recognisable shape. I have to admit that by now I was totally convulsed with laughter at this scene and had to remove myself from the area. The owner of the baby walker was justifiably very annoyed and was later recompensed for the damage, but for me the picture of my fellow crew members trying to sort out the 'metallic puzzle' remains one of my favourite and lasting airline memories.

Chilly in Milan

Hand baggage was always a thorny issue with cabin crew and often the cause of a great deal of aggravation, particularly when the passengers appeared at the aircraft laden down with bags.

42

The passengers were boarding in Milan for the homeward flight to London. Being the in-charge crew member, I was stationed at the forward main door of the aircraft. We had a full flight back to Heathrow and, as ever, there was the problem with stowing hand baggage (mention 'hand baggage' to any crew member, past or present, and watch their reaction, which will nearly always be the same one – exasperation!)

In the midst of boarding I received a call from the crew at the rear passenger door requesting my assistance. I arrived at the back of the aircraft to find that boarding had stopped. A member of the ground staff was trying to help a passenger pass through the door with his hand baggage and a refrigerator still in its box.

Not able to believe what I was witnessing, I asked the ground staff what he thought he was doing. He hurriedly explained that he was trying to help the customer with his hand baggage. I took a deep breath and asked where on board he proposed that we should stow this item and he suggested one of the toilets. After counting to ten, I told him to take the fridge away, as there was no way it was coming on board.

Unfortunately, the owner of the fridge and the ground staff thought that I was being very unreasonable, but needless to say the fridge remained in Milan while the customer travelled with us to LHR, sulking most of the way.

Is it Me, or Is it Hot?

I had been studying Spanish for a while as I loved (and still do) both Spain and the Spanish language, so at every opportunity when visiting the country I would try out my Spanish. I quickly learned that the Spanish people delight in foreigners who try to speak their language. If you happen to mispronounce any words, they are more than happy to help with corrections.

I was in Madrid on an aircraft that had come from and was about to return to London. We had a 45-minute turn round, so the aircraft was full of airline staff, cleaners and caterers, all preparing for the return flight. Being the middle of summer, the weather was very hot, and the temperature in the passenger cabin was rising, in spite of the aircraft's cooling system.

Keen to continue with my Spanish language practice, I approached one of the cleaning ladies and announced with a little too much confidence, 'Ola, tengo muy caliente – y usted?'

The lady took one look at me and burst into uncontrollable laughter, while inviting her colleagues to join us.

'Otra vez!' ('Again') she said, still giggling.

She was obviously well impressed, I thought, as I repeated how hot I felt. Now I had six Spanish cleaning ladies all hooting with laughter. Frankly, I wasn't impressed at their reaction, as I couldn't see the joke.

Hearing the commotion, a Spanish member of the ground staff came over to see what was going on, as by this time no one was doing any cleaning and the passengers were due at any minute.

'What exactly did you say?' he asked, so I repeated the sentence.

Now every Spanish person within earshot was laughing, while I stood feeling confused and embarrassed.

'You just told the cleaner and everyone else that you are feeling randy, not hot!'

Clearly more study and practice was needed.

Joan Collins

Over the years, I met many famous people, and here are stories about three of them.

The Tristar bound for Paris Charles de Gaulle had an indefinite delay. The aircraft was fully booked and the passengers were becoming fractious, as the delay was inevitably having an effect on any plans that they had made for their stay in Paris and their onward travel connections. One of the Business Class passengers that day happened to be Joan Collins, who was known for her frankness.

After 45 minutes, Miss Collins got out of her seat and came towards the front of the aircraft. Her reputation came before her, and it was with a certain amount of trepidation that I said to her, 'Can I help Miss Collins?'

She replied, 'Do you think that I could get off this aircraft and transfer to another carrier?'

I was astounded that she was being so nice and charming. The problem was that her request was exactly what most of the other passengers also wanted to ask, and if we allowed her to disembark there would be a stampede for the exit.

I felt that several hundred pairs of eyes and ears were watching and listening to my answer, so I took a deep breath and said, 'We don't expect

44

to be delayed for much longer, and if we let you disembark I'm afraid that the rest of the passengers will want to follow you.'

Her reply was 'I quite understand,' and she returned to her seat without another word.

Alex Higgins

The aircraft had been boarded and the cabin crew were walking through the aircraft, checking that all the passengers were seated with seat belts fastened and bags stowed away, ready for take off.

The stewardess suddenly came upon a passenger who clearly was not complying with the safety regulations, holding a slim case between his knees. She pounced and said to the passenger, 'I'm afraid you are going to have to put your fishing rod in the hat rack.'

The hapless passenger on this occasion was the professional snooker player Alex Higgins, and his so-called fishing rod happened to be his precious snooker cue.

Celebrity – Where?

'We must respect his privacy. He does *not* want to be recognised, so don't draw attention to him" said the aircraft dispatcher about the celebrity due to arrive.

Duly briefed, the crew awaited the VIP with a vague lack of interest, bordering on amusement at the usual hype often associated with certain celebrities.

When all the passengers had boarded and were in their seats, the VIP swept on board, wearing a hat, long coat and large sunglasses. With everyone watching, he proceeded to slowly remove his hat and sunglasses. Then he turned round, surveying the other passengers before taking his seat, by then having been recognised by all on board. This particular VIP was Jack Nicholson.

This Ham's Off!

We met many RAF crews around the world, and heard many of their funny stories, but the next one is one of my favourites.

A fully laden RAF Tristar was heading south, carrying troops to the Falkland Islands. Due to technical difficulties, it was forced to land in

South America. The aircraft was fixed and re-catered with civilian meals on trays instead of the usual RAF cardboard boxes. The loadmaster and his crew were giving out the trays, when one of the soldiers called out, 'Oy, mate! This 'am's off!'

The loadmaster outranked the soldier, and bristling at such familiarity replied, 'First of all, I am not your mate; and second, that's not ham it's smoked salmon!'

How I wish I had said that!

Airline Jokes and Quips

(Q) What do a stewardess and a cow pat have in common?
(A) As they get older, they become easier to pick up!

Flying over the North Pole one day, a passenger asked a steward, 'Say, what are those things down there that look like icebergs?'

The steward replied, 'Icebergs, sir.'

When opening a UHT long-life milk jigger provided on the meal tray, a passenger looked at the label and asked the crew member serving tea and coffee, 'Excuse me steward, what sort of an animal is a UHT?'

Passenger: 'Hey, miss, what time are we landing?'
Crew member: 'I'm not sure, but I do know that we'll run out of fuel in three hours' time.'

Condensation was an issue on the older aircraft (especially the Boeing 707), and often on descent the frozen liquid inside the skin of the fuselage would melt and water would drip from the ceiling and cascade down the walls. Nearly every time a passenger would, in a state of panic, ask from where the water was coming. They would always receive the same answer: 'So sorry, we haven't had time to dry out the life rafts since we last used them!'

When asked if he thought that his alcohol consumption was possibly bad for his health, a crew member replied that this was not the case, as alcohol was a preservative. Asked if he had a drink problem, the same person replied, 'No, I can always get one!'

The flight deck crew had the nickname of the Nigels, and their favourite starter for breakfast when airborne was a 'Nigelburger' which consisted of corn flakes topped with a sliced banana, swimming in milk. Well, they seemed to like it!

A 'no go' catering item was the pilots' cheese board. On nearly every flight part of the pre-take off checks was to ensure that the cheese board was in the galley, so to prevent unnecessary angst on the flight deck the cheese board would accompany their first hot drinks of the day.

It was considered to be a very unusual event if a pilot refused a hot drink, a theory that I once put to the test. On the flight in question, I gave all three members of the flight deck crew a hot drink as soon as they boarded the aircraft, and kept taking them hot drinks every 20 to 25 minutes. As far as I remember they asked me to stop after three hours of consuming liquids. They then spent the next two hours visiting the toilet.

Nose Wheel Roulette
Each crew member (including pilots) would pick a number with an arrow pointing down to the point where the nose wheel tyre touched the ground. Each person would then pay an agreed sum of money and the lucky one whose number was nearest to the ground after 'chocks on' would take the prize. To ensure fair play, the flight engineer and a member of the cabin crew would get off the aircraft together to see the result.

CHAPTER 5

The Cabin Crew Job

In spite of all the fun and laughs, there is a serious side to the role of being a cabin crew member.

The primary role of cabin crew was and still is, that of a safety officer in the event of a medical or operational emergency on board. However, BA is a business which has survived until today by having both a viable route network and top quality customer service delivered by its front line staff, both on the ground and in the air.

To monitor service standards on board their flight, customers were randomly selected throughout the aircraft and given a customer satisfaction survey to complete. In addition, the customers were surveyed again in the arrivals hall, as they waited for their bags.

We were assigned our work by a crew scheduler who worked as part of the operations department, and the crew were then sent their trip roster in the post. In those days, the schedulers endeavoured to have the crew rosters posted out 28 days in advance, and there would be much wailing if the rosters were not out on time. The schedulers were very important to the crew, and it paid to build some sort of relationship with them, as they held the power to send the crew to virtually anywhere in the network. The rosters were very important, as the crews' salary varied according to where they went in the world.

The length of the long haul trips could be anything from three to 21 days. The three-day trips were to the east coast of the USA, Canada and the Gulf region. The 21 day trips sent their crews round the world.

My first round the world trip was to New York, Los Angeles, Honolulu, Fiji, Sydney, Auckland, Brisbane, Singapore, Sri Lanka, Nairobi and London. This trip was known as 'Sydney through the West', and was on a VC10. On this itinerary, our time off varied from 18 to 48 hours. It all depended on when the next aircraft arrived.

The number of days off at home earned after a trip depended upon how long the crew member had been away. So a three-day trip would earn three local nights, and a 21-day trip seven local nights. Those who produced the flying rosters tried not to schedule any crew member more than 180 days out of the country a year.

As long as the trip was on schedule all went well, but if there were delays or cancellations due to war, weather or technical problems then anything could happen. It was said (truthfully) that once you were off-schedule then you could go into orbit, and often this was the case. Once I was scheduled a three-day trip, and due to the second Arab/Israel war I came home 25 days later! The downside of the cabin crew role was that it could cause carnage to social events and relationships at home.

To cover for these disruptions, every four to six months long-haul crew were rostered a 28-day block of stand-by duties. This consisted of 48 hours at 90-minutes availability, which meant that the person called out had to be at the crew reporting centre ready for service 90 minutes from the call. After the 90-minute standby was finished there would be 12 hours off, after which the length of standby went to four and then to 12 hours. Generally, it was better to be called out sooner, as it cut down the waiting time. It is true to say that most crew disliked the 28 day block of stand-by, as it was impossible to plan anything at home for some weeks.

Crew who could speak a language found that they could be limited to visiting the same part of the world. French speakers were often to be found on the Canadian routes, and Spanish speakers would be sent to South America and the Caribbean. For routes to the Far East there were national girls from India, Hong Kong and Japan. These girls would wear their national dress, and looked stunning in their saris and kimonos.

Those flying just on European routes had a different rostering system. The great thing about short haul flying was that there was a fixed pattern of six days on and three days off. This work schedule was set in stone, which made it much easier to plan a life in the UK.

The short haul crew were rostered 28 days in advance and would get a day's stand-by, which would be done in the crew report centre at Heathrow. Their stand-by lasted six hours, and they would be in their uniform and ready to go at a minute's notice.

To be a cabin crew member you need to like people and want to help them, be empathic, work well under pressure, display a good sense of humour and enjoy working as part of a team. It was also said that the 'perfect' stewardess had the following qualities:

- The body of a race horse
- The strength of a cart horse
- The brains of a rocking horse.

I never heard what the requirements were for the perfect steward!

CHAPTER 6

Security

We live in a time where there is a constant threat to our security when we take to the air – a fear endorsed by the events of the 11th September, 2001. In fact the hijacking of aircraft started in the early 70s, and by today's standards was a regular occurrence.

On the 6th September, 1970, two aircraft were hijacked by Palestinian militants and taken to Dawsons Field, a disused RAF airfield in the Jordanian dessert – a Swissair DC-8 and a TWA Boeing 707. There had been previous failed hijack attempts on two other aircraft. On the 9th September three Palestinians took control of a BOAC Super VC10 (GASGN), which was taken to join the other two aircraft at Dawsons Field.

On the 11th September all of the hostages were taken to the capital of Jordan, Amman. They were all released except for 35 men and five women, who were hidden in a secret location in Amman. These remaining hostages were kept to secure the release of Palestinian dissidents who were being held by other countries.

The three planes on the ground at Dawsons Field. [British Airways Heritage Centre]

On the 12th September the three aircraft at Dawsons Field were destroyed with explosives. After lengthy negotiations a deal was struck, and on the 30th September the hostages were finally freed.

The next incident occurred on the 3rd of March 1974 when another BOAC Super VC10 (GASGO) was hijacked and taken to Amsterdam. After releasing the hostages, the hijackers set fire to the aircraft using alcohol from the First Class bar – a terrible waste of ship's stores!

On another occasion, in November 1974, a VC10 was on the tarmac in Dubai when it was stormed by hijackers. As they rushed the aircraft the hijackers were firing their weapons and hit a stewardess in the back – a wound from which she fortunately recovered.

One of the stewards had a lucky escape as he was leaving the aircraft. Walking towards the terminal he felt as if something had flicked his shirt, and on looking down he noticed a bullet hole. The bullet had missed him by inches.

View of the three destroyed aircraft from the air. [British Airways Heritage Centre]

The hijackers didn't realise that there were no pilots on board to fly the aircraft, but knowing that there were terrorists waiting for them Captain Jim Futcher and his crew boarded the aircraft and flew it to Tripoli to be refuelled. From there they flew on to Tunis, where a hostage was murdered by the hijackers, before they eventually surrendered after 84 hours.

Captain Futcher was later awarded the Queen's Gallantry Medal.

During this time Athens became a bit of a 'hot spot' and a cartoon at the time showed a terrorist buying a six-pack of hand grenades in the duty free shop.

To counter the threat posed by these ruthless people, security officers were stationed at destinations where the risk of hijack was high. It was their job to identify areas where the security was lax, and to work with the local airport, police and security services to improve the situation.

CHAPTER 7

A Hurricane, an Earthquake
and an Emergency

During years of travelling the world and logging many millions of air miles, there were three occasions when I felt that things were about to go very wrong indeed.

Two were caused by natural phenomena, which demonstrated the power of Mother Nature. The other was a result of a technical fault with the aircraft.

Hurricane Allen – St Lucia

The crew of the Boeing 707 (two pilots, one flight engineer, six cabin crew) had ended their three days off in St Lucia and were due to return to London Heathrow on the evening of 3rd August, 1980.

All day on the island's radio there had been warnings of the approach of the first hurricane of the season, Hurricane Allen. (As the first one, it was to be given a boy's name starting with the letter A, which progressed through the alphabet, as the hurricane season continued). We hoped that the aircraft, which was due from Antigua, would land to pick us up before the airport closed as a result of the deteriorating weather.

The crew gathered in the hotel lobby to be picked up and driven to Hewanorra Airport with the weather worsening all the while – heavy downpours and an increasing wind. On arrival at the airport we were told that we had a 'full house' of passengers and needed to depart as soon as possible.

The captain went up into the airport control tower to look at the weather radar, where he saw a vast circle of cloud clearly showing the hurricane advancing ominously towards the island of St Lucia. Winds were forecast to be in excess of 100mph, accompanied by a tidal surge.

By this time, the winds over St Lucia were too strong for the incoming aircraft to land. It diverted to Barbados, where the weather was also bad, but still within the aircraft's limits to land. The winds at Hewanorra airport were now over 70mph, so we made our way back to the hotels (together with our London-bound passengers), where it was planned that we would ride out the storm.

The hotel was now full, and once the two female crew and passengers had been allocated rooms, all that was left for the male crew members was a beach house in the hotel grounds, on stilts and surrounded by palm trees.

Our bags were brought to the beach house, along with three cases of beer, 18 cokes and four bottles of local dark rum, with the instructions that under no circumstances were we to leave the building – no matter what happened.The engineer had previously been caught in a hurricane and he said that we were in for a night that we would never forget.

So we prepared for the onslaught by pouring out and sampling the rum, which we washed down with the beers which had kindly been given to us. Suddenly we heard, 'Come and look at this!' We ran to the door, through which we could see palm trees being effortlessly ripped out of the ground

St Lucia, still windy the morning after Hurricane Allen.

and flying in all directions. At that point, all the light and power went off. We went carefully back into the house and talked through a strategy should things go seriously wrong. It became clear to us that the centre of the hurricane was now coming our way – the wind was so loud that talking or even shouting to each other was futile, and our ears were popping as the pressure dropped like a stone.

Then suddenly, it stopped and all went still – we were in the eye of the storm. It was bizarre, as one could still see stars in the sky at that point.

This situation continued for about twenty minutes, after which the strong winds returned from another direction, blowing just as hard, along with more torrential rain. Then suddenly and with a large crash, part of the roof of our beach house was ripped off and blown away and the house itself started to lift up off the ground – which was not a good situation.

While this was going on there were continuous crashing sounds caused, as we later found out, by uprooted palm trees hitting our fragile building. Not for the first time in my life I thought, 'This is it.'

I seem to remember that I sheltered under a table while water poured into our flimsy shelter. The storm continued unabated through the night.

Eventually I fell asleep and was woken by warm sunshine pouring into what was left of our beach house. Still under the table, I realised that I was lying in a pool of water. On what was left of the veranda sat the other six crew, all looking somewhat dazed and dishevelled.

I went outside to see a scene of complete devastation, but by some piece of luck, our building had survived due to the fact that the palm trees had been stacked up to roof level by the storm, so offering our house a natural protection from the elements. Without this good fortune, our situation would have been critical.

As I surveyed what we nicknamed 'The Windy Wendy House', I was approached by a St Lucian who said to me, 'Were you in there, man?'

'Yes,' I replied.

The man just looked at me and announced, 'Praise the Lord! Praise the Lord!'

I can remember that night as if it had happened yesterday.

It wasn't until sometime later that the facts associated with Hurricane Allen were published.
- The hurricane killed at least 271 people in the Caribbean area.
- 18 people were killed in St.Lucia.
- It decimated the output of the island's agriculture.
- In total it caused $2.6 billion worth of damage.
- It was the strongest hurricane of the 1980 season.
- It was the earliest ever recorded Category 5 hurricane (winds in excess of 155 mph with a tidal surge in excess of 18 feet).
- At its peak the winds were recorded at 190mph.
- It is the fifth most powerful storm on record.
- Throughout the night Radio St.Lucia made public service broadcasts playing 'appropriate' music such as 'Blowing in the wind' and 'As you walk through a storm'.
- The next morning there were still waves of up to 30ft rolling in to Castries harbour in the north of the Island.

An Earthquake

Nature once again showed her power, this time using an earthquake to show who was in charge. I can still hear that rumbling sound, and feel the ground moving underfoot.

Our aircraft landed very early on New Year's Eve in Anchorage, Alaska. After a few post flight drinks in the hotel, we agreed to meet up in the lobby later before going on to a party thrown by a member of the Anchorage airport ground staff.

Anchorage is set at the end of the San Andreas Belt, and it had been very badly hit by a severe earthquake on Good Friday, 1964, so we had been discussing what to do in the event of one striking while we were staying there.

The general consensus was that you should open your hotel room door and stand under the door's lintel. About an hour before we were due to meet I had just stepped out of the shower and walked from the bathroom to the bedroom. As I went to sit on the bed, there was a tremendous jolt – the bed moved and I fell onto the floor. I had no idea what was happening, but I got up from the floor and continued drying myself.

After a minute or so there was another massive jolt, and this time the room started to sway from side to side – there was no doubt that this was a significant earthquake. It was now difficult to stand, so I got onto my hands and knees and crawled to the door, which I managed to open with a certain amount of difficulty. I positioned myself at the door, wearing just a towel, and took stock of the situation. In doorways up and down the corridor, were my colleagues in various states of undress, either screaming or giggling.

One of these colleagues called out to us helpfully, 'You realise that if the hotel falls down we will have very little hope of survival, as the outside temperature is -20 degrees centigrade, plus the wind chill.'

We laughed, nervously.

Thankfully, the hotel did not fall down, but there was damage sustained to buildings that night in and around the town. For two days afterwards there were significant aftershocks and I was never more pleased to leave anywhere than when our flight took off for London. For me, it still remains a terrifying but memorable experience.

When researching the facts and dates of incidents, I could find nothing about the earthquake in Anchorage other than the one in 1964. At the time it seemed severe. There were warnings put out on the radio about the need to conserve water, and a message from the governor. But it would seem that it was nothing to the tough Alaskans, and not even worth a mention.

An Emergency

It is said that from the point of view of a pilot, flying is 99 per cent boredom and 1 per cent terror. I feel sure that the flight crew involved in this incident would agree, because at the time my hair was standing on end!

We were leaving Panama with a very light load of passengers, and for the sake of the balance of the aircraft most of them were seated either over the wing, or forward of it. We were on a Boeing 707, and my crew seat, which was shared with another crew member, was positioned by the two rear door exits of the aircraft.

I duly took my seat as the aircraft began to roll down the runway. It quickly gathered speed, but as its nose lifted off the ground there was a tremendous bang. The aircraft lurched to the right and the outboard engine went into spin and rinse. Flames poured from the engine as the captain somehow prevented the wing from hitting the ground. He then regained control and the automatic fire extinguishers put out the fire. However, the aircraft still had a full load of fuel on board, and this could not be dumped for fear of re-igniting the engine.

We circled the airfield and came in to land, having briefed the passengers for a possible emergency evacuation. The aircraft made a perfect landing and, escorted by the airport fire engines, we taxied in to the terminal building.

After an engine change, the aircraft was as good as new, as if nothing had happened. The captain and his team on the flight deck that day thought that they had done nothing other than their job.

In 1988 I moved to another position within the airline, this time managing people. It was still fun, but I missed being part of the crew. However, I had had enough of permanently living out of a suitcase and being away from home.

CHAPTER 8

Sounds of the Seventies

The Boys of BOAC
– sung to the tune of Old King Cole

Now Captain Cole was a merry olde soul and a merry olde soul was he,
He called for his pipe in the middle of the night and he called for his pilots
    three,
Now every pilot was a fine chap, and a very fine chap was he.

'I don't give a damn!' said the pilots,
   Merry, merry men are we,
   There's none so fair as can compare
   With the boys of BOAC!

'Da-Di-Di, Da-Di-Di, Da', said the R/O [radio officer],

'Ten thousand pounds of thrust!' said the engineer,

'Fifty miles off track!' said the navigator,

'I've written off the whole bloody bar!' said the purser,

'My oven's [or Macro, for the purist] blown a fuse,' said the steward,

'Do you want it up the back or up the front?' said the stewardess,

   Merry, merry men are we,
   There's none so fair as can compare
   [Big finish] *With the boys of BOAC!*

Lament of the VC10

– sung to the tune of My Bonnie Lies Over the Ocean

My bomber flies over the ocean,
My bomber flies over the sea,
My bomber flies over the ocean,
Bring back VC10s just for me.

Chorus:
Bring back, Oh bring back,
Bring back VC10s just for me, for me.
Bring back, Oh bring back,
Bring back VC10s just for me.

My bomber flies over the ocean,
My bomber flies over the sea,
On Jumbos [747s] you get no promotion.
Bring back VC10s just for me.

Chorus:
Bring back, Oh bring back,
Bring back VC10s just for me, for me.
Bring back, Oh bring back,
Bring back VC10s just for me.

This book is also available as an audio download.

For further details, and to listen to the free sampler, visit our website:
www.airlinehumour.co.uk